SUPERHERO PETS

True Tales of Animal Heroes

SUPERHERO PETS

True Tales of Animal Heroes

Joanne Mattern

SCHOLASTIC INC.

ISBN 978-0-545-46042-2

12 11 10 9 8 7 6 5 4 3 2 1   12 13 14 15 16 17/0

Printed in the U.S.A.   40
First Scholastic printing, September 2012

To all my pets past and present, superheroes in their own way.

—JM

Contents

HEROES IN ALL SHAPES AND SIZES

Pets are wonderful companions, and sometimes they also are heroes. Some pets have rushed to help when the person they loved was injured or in danger. Other pets have saved neighbors and people they didn't even know.

Dogs and cats can be assistance or therapy pets, helping people perform everyday tasks or bringing comfort to a person who is sick or lonely. Pet heroes come in all shapes and sizes, from tiny kittens and puppies to horses, pigs, and cows. Even wild animals have been heroes.

What makes a pet perform a lifesaving deed? Some people say that animals are just trying to save themselves when they warn people about a fire or other danger. But others believe that animals are compassionate. They care about people and do their best to help when scary things happen.

Pet heroes have rescued people in amazing ways. From the dog who saved his owner from choking to the cat who dialed 911 when his owner had a seizure, pets and other animals are capable of almost anything! Each story is based on a true-life event, but some have been dramatized with re-created dialogue. In some cases, the names and places have been changed. So settle back, turn the page, and meet an astonishing collection of superhero pets!

CHAPTER 1

FIRE AND OTHER DANGERS

When a home catches fire or fills with deadly carbon monoxide gas, every second counts. The superhero pets in this chapter didn't waste any time getting their owners out of danger. Thanks to them, entire families were saved from disastrous situations.

THREE-LEGGED RESCUE

When Mary and John Smith, an elderly couple living in Independence County, Arkansas, adopted a five-year-old rat terrier from a shelter, they saved her life. No one else wanted the three-legged dog, who was scheduled to be euthanized. Mary and John loved their little dog, whom they named Tripod because she had only three legs. They had no idea that Tripod would return the favor and save *their* lives.

Late one night, about a year after the Smiths adopted Tripod, the little dog woke up from her spot at the foot of their bed. She smelled smoke. The house was on fire! Tripod barked to awaken her owners, staying close by even as the flames reached the couple's bed.

Mary woke up in the burning bedroom and struggled to get up. Her husband, who was disabled and unable to walk, lay helplessly in bed beside her. "I couldn't imagine how I could get John and myself out of that room," Mary said. She gave up and lay back down. "I accepted our fate. We were going to die together."

But Tripod was not going to let Mary and John die. The little dog kept barking and pulling at their clothes, trying to drag them out of bed despite her tiny size and missing leg. Finally, Mary decided that if the disabled dog could keep going, she could, too. She managed to get herself and John out of the house before it burned down. "There's only one reason John and I are alive today, and that's Tripod," Mary said.

THE NEW ARRIVAL

When Daniel and Tracie Giffin's three children, Cole, Spencer, and Sarah, went to pick out a new puppy, no one would have imagined that the pup they chose would save their lives that very same night. They chose a twelve-week-old dog and named him Schmichael. The puppy joined their other dog and two cats as a member of the family.

Tracie let the children stay up late that night to play with their new pet, but she finally sent everyone off to their rooms to bed. When Daniel came home late that night from work, everyone was asleep. Daniel checked on Schmichael, who was sound asleep in his crate in the bedroom, then climbed into bed himself. Tired from the long day, he quickly fell asleep.

In the middle of the night, Schmichael began whimpering. The puppy's cries woke up Daniel. "Shhh, it's okay," he whispered, thinking the dog was just scared and lonely in his new home. But the puppy continued to whine and cry. Daniel realized something was wrong. Schmichael was clearly agitated and trying to get the attention of his new owners.

Daniel climbed out of bed and looked out of the window. "Oh, no!" he yelled. The barn just behind the house was on fire, with the wind whipping flames high into the night sky. "Tracie! Wake up!" he yelled. "The barn's on fire!" Tracie and Daniel rushed to wake their children and gather the family pets, including Schmichael. As Tracie, the children, and their pets hurried outside, Daniel called 911.

Firefighters arrived quickly and tried their best to save the house, but there was nothing they could do. The family watched in disbelief as everything they owned was destroyed by the fire. The flames took their home and their possessions, but everyone in the family was safe, thanks to Schmichael. "Call it fate, call it coincidence," said Daniel. "But in less than twenty-four hours of coming into our lives, Schmichael helped save us."

JELLIE JILL SAVES THE DAY

When Caroline McColl adopted her cairn terrier, Jellie Jill, she could not have guessed that Jellie Jill would become such a great helper. Caroline had serious health problems caused by multiple strokes. The strokes had left her partly blind, and she had trouble walking. She also suffered from severe headaches called migraines.

To her surprise, Caroline found that Jellie Jill could predict when a migraine was about to happen. When she sensed a migraine coming, Jellie Jill would pull at her pant leg until she lay down. Then the little dog sat beside her to keep her company until Caroline felt better. Jellie Jill also saved her life several times by barking and pulling on her leash to keep Caroline from walking in front of moving vehicles she couldn't see. But that was nothing compared to what Jellie Jill did in March 2004.

On one fateful afternoon, Caroline turned on the oven in her apartment to start dinner, then lay down on her bed to rest. She meant to rest for only a few minutes, but instead, she fell asleep. The next thing she remembered was Jellie Jill nipping at her, licking her face, and jumping up and down on the bed wildly. "How did you get up here?" Caroline asked in surprise. Her bed was elevated to make it easier for her to get in and out, and the little terrier hadn't been able to get up there before.

"What's the matter, Jellie Jill?" Caroline asked. Then she heard a popping sound from the kitchen. She hurried to see what was wrong. To her horror, she saw that the stove was on fire and an entire wall in the kitchen was blazing.

Caroline grabbed her little dog hero and rushed outside. The fire department arrived and put out the fire before it could spread to other parts of the building. "If your dog hadn't alerted you, the whole building could have burned down," a firefighter told her.

Caroline knew the firefighter was right. "If Jellie had not woken me that afternoon, I wouldn't be here," she said. "She is my hero, my angel, and my best friend."

A SILENT KILLER

Janet and John Walderbach had enjoyed a pleasant day with their guests, and everyone was tired out by the evening. Janet put the two young children to bed, and she and John went to sleep soon afterward. The house was warm and cozy, thanks to the heat from their furnace. But something else was spreading through their home — deadly carbon monoxide gas. You can't see or smell carbon monoxide, but it can kill a person if he or she breathes too much of it.

In the middle of the night, the children woke up and began to cry. Janet rocked one of them back to sleep, then lay down on their bed. She didn't feel well and could hardly keep her eyes open. *I'll just sleep here for a little while,* she decided as she dozed off.

Janet had only been asleep for a few minutes when she felt the cold, wet nose of Shelby, the family's German shepherd, pushing against her face. The dog was whining and pacing around the bed.

Janet sat up, but she felt worse than ever. She stumbled back to her bed and woke her husband. "I feel awful," he said. "I feel like I'm going to be sick."

"Me, too," Janet said. "Shelby, stop!" The dog was still whining and pushing at her. "She probably wants a walk." John led Shelby to the door and pushed her outside into the yard.

Being outside alone was not what Shelby wanted. As soon as John shut the door, the big dog began barking and scratching at it. When Janet opened it, the dog kept barking, staring at her, and backing up, then walking forward and barking some more.

"I think something's wrong," Janet said. "Get the kids and let's get outside." John hurried to grab the children, and everyone rushed into the cold night air. Shelby immediately stopped barking and wagged her tail.

"I don't feel good," one of the children whimpered.

"That does it," John said. "We're going to the hospital." They piled into the car and drove to the nearest emergency room. Doctors discovered everyone was suffering from carbon monoxide poisoning, because the furnace was not working right. Later, investigators found that the level of carbon monoxide in their home was so high, they would have died if they'd stayed inside any longer.

When the Skippy Dog Food Company heard about Shelby's lifesaving actions, they named her its Dog Hero of the Year. Shelby was awarded five hundred dollars, a year's supply of food, and an engraved bowl. Most of all, Shelby won the gratitude and continued love of the people whose lives she saved on that cold winter night.

A LITTLE DOG SAVES A BIG FAMILY

Even a little dog can be a big hero. Linda and James Clevenger of Bremen, Indiana, found that out one cold winter night. The couple and their five children were sleeping soundly on February 2, 2005. Two of their daughters, twelve-year-old Katrina and sixteen-year-old Kelli, were sleeping in their bunk beds in the room they shared. Katrina's miniature dachshund, Maggie, was snuggled into the top bunk with Katrina.

Suddenly, Maggie started barking and jumping up and down. Her barking woke Kelli. Thinking the dog just needed to go outside, she reached up and lifted her down to the floor. Maggie ran out of the room, and Kelli drifted back to sleep.

Maggie ran to the bedroom that Linda and James shared, but the door was closed. Still barking, she pawed and scratched at the door. Finally, the little dog managed to push it open. She ran to the bed, barking and jumping at the covers, until Linda at last got up. "What's the matter with you, Maggie?" she asked. "You never get up during the night."

Still barking, Maggie ran into the kitchen. Linda followed. As soon as she walked in the room, she realized something was terribly wrong. Someone had accidentally left on one of the stove's burners, and natural gas was filling the room. Linda's hand reached for the light switch, then stopped. The spark from the light could set off an explosion!

Instead, Linda rushed to turn off the gas and open the windows, gagging on the sickening smell. Then she and James woke the rest of the family and led them outside to safety. "Maggie is our hero," Linda said. "Thanks to her, there was no headline in the paper: 'House Explodes, Killing Family of Seven.'"

A CELEBRITY HERO

Pets who belong to celebrities are often in the news, photographed with their owners playing on the beach or shopping. But Flossie, a yellow Lab and chow mix who belonged to actress Drew Barrymore and her then fiancé, comedian Tom Green, became a celebrity herself for a much more important reason. She saved Drew's and Tom's lives.

Drew and Tom were asleep in their house in Beverly Hills, one night in February 2001. About three o'clock in the morning, Flossie woke them up with her frantic barking and jumping. She "literally banged on their bedroom door." When Drew and Tom got up, they discovered the house was on fire. Because of Flossie's alert, they were able to escape the fire, along with Flossie and their other pets. The house was completely destroyed, but no one was hurt.

Perhaps Flossie was just returning the favor. Drew had adopted the stray dog two years earlier when they met on the street. That was probably the best decision Drew ever made!

SUPER KITTY!

Cats can be heroes, too. Cathy and Eric Keesling and their family were asleep at home in New Castle, Indiana, one night in March 2007, when a gasoline-powered water pump in the basement malfunctioned. Carbon monoxide began filling the house. The sleeping family had no way of knowing what was happening — until Winnie the cat saved the day.

Somehow, Winnie sensed something was wrong. She jumped on Cathy and Eric's bed and began meowing loudly in Cathy's ear. "It was a crazy meow, almost like she was screaming," Cathy recalled.

Finally, Cathy got up. She felt dizzy and sick. When she tried to wake her husband, Eric wouldn't wake up. Cathy realized something bad was happening and called 911. When the fire department arrived, they found the couple's teenage son, Michael, unconscious on the floor of his room. The family was taken outside and given oxygen until they recovered.

Winnie escaped with the family, and everyone survived their encounter with a silent killer. Cathy told reporters that Winnie had acted the same way half a year earlier when tornadoes passed through the area. "I really believe cats can sense these kinds of things," she said. Winnie was honored as Cat of the Year by the ASPCA in 2007.

SAMANTHA SAVES THEM ALL

Tia Jenkins called a little black cat named Samantha her "angel kitty." Tia was disabled because of vision problems and seizures. She got the cat from a neighbor who didn't want her anymore — the neighbor threatened to kill the cat if someone didn't take her, so Tia had to step in. At first, she did not intend to keep Samantha, but the kitten made her laugh and kept her company. She trained Samantha to fetch things for her and to alert someone if she had a seizure.

Tia had just moved into an apartment in Louisville, Kentucky, and in January 2004, she heard a funny noise in the kitchen and went to check. Suddenly, Samantha began meowing loudly. Tia realized that the kitchen stove had caught fire. The apartment filled with smoke, making it almost impossible for her to see. She quickly called 911 and was told to leave the apartment right away. She would not leave without Samantha or her pet turtle, Shelly. But how could she find them in the smoke-filled apartment?

Tia heard Samantha crying and clawing at the glass of Shelly's aquarium. She made her way to the aquarium, scooped out the turtle, and placed her in her purse. Then she heard Samantha meowing again. Tia followed the sound and found Samantha waiting by her carrier. She quickly pushed the cat inside and brought the carrier outside. "Later, the firefighters told me that by the time the smoke detector sounded, the whole kitchen would have gone up in flames," Tia said. "If it had not been for

Samantha's warning and bravery, none of us would be here today."

Tia wanted Samantha to be recognized for her actions. Most of all, she wanted to make sure that Samantha would stay with her as long as she lived. In August 2004, the state of Kentucky recognized Samantha as a service animal because of the many ways in which she helped Tia. The recognition meant that Samantha was protected under the law and would always be Tia's "angel kitty."

COLD-WEATHER HERO

Geppetto was just a little orange kitten when he became a part of the Sjogren family in Wetaskiwin, Canada. The years passed, and Geppetto grew into a relaxed cat who rarely meowed or looked for attention. That's why his amazing behavior one night in December 2009 was a life-saving surprise.

The weather had been cold and snowy all weekend. Phyllis Sjogren didn't want to get out of her warm bed on Monday morning, even when her husband, Martin, left for work. She was not only cold, but she'd had a bad headache all night. So she stayed in bed until six thirty in the morning. That's when a terrible wailing woke her.

"I knew it was Geppetto crying, but I'd never heard him make that noise before," Phyllis said. Despite her headache, which was even worse now, she made her way into the kitchen. There, she found Geppetto standing at the top of the basement stairs, screaming and meowing.

Phyllis felt dizzy and nauseated, and her headache was pounding. She called her husband to tell him what was happening and was shocked when he said, "Get out of that house *now*!" She scooped up Geppetto and hurried outside while Martin called the gas company. Emergency workers discovered that the house was full of carbon monoxide from a faulty furnace. Phyllis was treated for severe carbon monoxide poisoning, but she and Geppetto recovered. Geppetto went back to his quiet ways after the incident, but Phyllis and Martin Sjogren will never forget the morning he used his voice to save his owner.

CHAPTER 2

PETS TO THE RESCUE!

From pulling a man out of an icy pond to saving a girl from a deer attack, the superhero pets in this chapter have saved the day! It doesn't matter if they are dogs, cats, horses, or even cows — these pets were there when their owners needed them most.

BOOMER LEADS THE WAY

Bobbie Glover was enjoying an afternoon walk with Boomer, her five-year-old Labrador retriever. Boomer had been a beloved family pet since the Glovers adopted him from a shelter a few years earlier. Their Auburn, California, neighborhood was quiet, with most families at work or at school, and Bobbie did not see anyone as they walked along.

As Bobbie crossed the street, she was busy looking at a nearby garden instead of where she was going. Suddenly, she tripped and both feet caught the edge of a pothole in the road. Her legs twisted and she fell hard. Pain shot up both legs. She knew she was badly hurt. She couldn't walk or even stand up. Boomer stood next to her, whining. When she didn't get up, the big dog lay down next to her in the road.

"Help!" Bobbie yelled. "Somebody help me!" But there was no answer in the quiet neighborhood. She knew she needed to get home. But how? She realized that Boomer was her only hope.

Bobbie wrapped her arms around Boomer's neck. "Home," she said. Boomer got up and began dragging her down the street. He stopped occasionally, but she urged him on. Finally, the two of them made it back to her house. Boomer ran to the door and barked as she yelled for help. Bobbie's husband rushed outside and found her. He called an ambulance and she was rushed to the hospital. She discovered she had two broken legs. "I had rescued Boomer from a shelter. I never dreamed he would end up rescuing me," Bobbie said.

NOT AFRAID OF ANYTHING

Herding cattle was an everyday job on the Mosher family ranch in Cherhill, Canada. So no one expected anything out of the ordinary to happen when Glenda and Gary Mosher and their eleven-year-old grandson, Travis, went out to check on their cows after dinner one March evening in 2010. The Moshers' two dogs, Scooter, an old Australian cattle dog, and Missy, a border collie, tagged along.

When the Moshers arrived at the field, they saw that a few of their neighbor's cows had gotten into their herd. Gary went to open the gate while Glenda, Travis, and the dogs walked into the herd and began to direct the three visiting cows toward the gate. Two of the cows ambled through the gate without any problem. But as the third cow went through, she turned back toward Glenda and knocked her down, then struck the woman's body over and over with her powerful hooves.

Gary was too far away to help, and Travis was so scared, all he could do was scream. That's when Scooter and Missy jumped into action. Scooter jumped at the cow's head and bit her on the nose. Missy darted behind the cow and bit her hind leg. The dogs kept on biting and jumping at the cow until the big animal finally turned and ran away.

Gary rushed to Glenda's side and sent Travis to the house to call for help. Scooter and Missy stayed close by until an ambulance arrived to take Glenda to the hospital. She was badly hurt, with broken bones and head injuries. She spent a month in the hospital, but she finally recovered and was able to return home. Glenda never would have survived without Scooter's and Missy's quick actions.

CHILD IN DANGER!

The Sararas family of Trenton, Canada, chose a whippet as their first dog because they heard that the breed was smart. Little Moose joined the family when he was only six weeks old. It was merely a few months later when Moose showed his family just how smart and heroic he was.

Jolene dropped her son off at school and then returned home, one day in April 2010. When she got home, her three-year-old daughter, Alexis, went outside to play with Moose in the family's fenced yard. "I'll be right out," Jolene told her. "I just need to load the dishwasher." She left the back door open to keep an eye on Alexis.

A few moments later, Moose ran inside and stared at Jolene. Then he ran outside. When Jolene didn't follow, he ran inside again and gave her the same puzzling look, then ran outside and started barking. She looked out and saw that Moose was jumping up and down. Moose had never behaved that way before, so she went out to see what was going on. She was greeted by a horrible sight. Alexis had tried to open the gate, when it swung shut instead, trapping her neck between two metal bars. The little girl was lying on the ground, with her body on one side of the gate and her head on the other.

Jolene quickly freed her daughter's head, but Alexis was limp and barely breathing. Jolene called 911. Alexis was rushed to the hospital, where she made a full recovery. Other than a bad bruise on her neck, the little girl was fine. And Moose got a new nickname from his grateful family. They now called him "Moose the Wonder Dog."

ONE SMART KITTY

Many people think you can't train a cat, but Gary Rosheisen of Columbus, Ohio, would say they're wrong. Gary was disabled. He couldn't walk and used a wheelchair to get around. He'd also suffered several strokes, which made his health even more fragile. Despite his disabilities, he felt safe living alone with his pet cat, Tommy.

Gary knew it was important for him to call for medical help quickly if he needed it, so he took several precautions. He set 911 on speed dial on his phone, installed a cord above his pillow that allowed him to contact the paramedics, and wore a medical-alert necklace every day. He even tried to teach Tommy how to call 911, although the cat didn't seem interested. His friends told him that was a silly idea, and Gary figured they were probably right.

One morning, Gary was getting out of bed when he fell out of his wheelchair. He hadn't put on his medical-alert necklace yet and couldn't reach his phone or the paramedic pull cord above his bed.

"Help! Help! Can anyone hear me?" Gary yelled. His only reply was silence. Without the strength to get up or even move, he gave up and lay on the floor. There was no one to rescue him.

Gary was wrong. Some time later, police burst into his apartment. They got him back into his wheelchair and made sure he was okay. "How did you know I needed help?" Gary asked. "Did a neighbor call you?"

"Not a neighbor," said a police officer. "We received a nine-one-one call from this apartment. No one spoke during the call, but we were able to track the address and came to check if everything was okay."

"But there's no one here except me, and I couldn't reach the phone," Gary said, puzzled.

"No one?" The police officer looked around. "That's funny. Someone called us from this address!"

Just then Gary saw Tommy sitting in the corner of the room, watching him. Gary smiled. The police might not believe him, but Gary knew who had made that lifesaving phone call. It seemed that teaching Tommy to dial 911 had paid off after all.

DON'T COME ANY CLOSER!

It might not surprise you that a dog or cat can save its owner from danger, but how about a cow? Janice Wolf found that idea hard to believe . . . until the day an eleven-month-old calf named Lurch saved her life.

Janice ran an animal refuge in Arkansas that included

large herds of longhorn cattle. One day, she was walking through the back pasture of her refuge when one of her calves blocked her path. "Lurch, get out of my way," Janice told the calf, but the big animal refused to move.

"Come on, Lurch. I have work to do. Move it!" she said, but Lurch stood firm. She grabbed the bull's horns and tried to push him out of the way, but he just shook her off with a snort and pawed at the ground.

Janice looked down — and froze in horror. Hiding in the grass, exactly where she was about to step, was a copperhead snake. Copperheads are poisonous. A bite from a copperhead could have killed Janice, who was especially sensitive to venom. Before she could move, Lurch ran forward and stomped on the snake until it was dead.

"Thank you, Lurch," Janice whispered, shaking, as she carefully backed away from the deadly danger that had been hiding in the grass.

THE FEARLESS CHIHUAHUA

Even little dogs can be big heroes. Zoey the Chihuahua weighed fewer than five pounds, but her tiny size didn't stop her from performing a big deed.

One hot summer day in 2007, Zoey was playing in the backyard with owner Marty Long and his baby grandson, Booker West. Without any warning, Zoey suddenly ran at the one-year-old. Marty was surprised. Then he was horrified. As he watched, a rattlesnake lunged out of the grass and bit Zoey on the face. The little dog had gotten between Booker and the snake just seconds before the snake would have bitten the baby. Rattlesnakes are one of the most poisonous kinds of snakes, and a bite from one could have killed Booker.

Zoey ran back to Marty, crying. Within minutes, her head swelled up to the size of a grapefruit. Marty rushed the little dog to the vet, where she was given special anti-venom and medicine. Zoey made a full recovery, but she had a one-inch scar on her face as a result of her lifesaving action.

IN AND OUT OF TROUBLE

Paul Walker's dog, Foster, got him into big trouble one night. Luckily for Paul, Foster did a great job of getting Paul *out* of trouble as well.

The high school senior was taking Foster for a walk through their Tallahassee, Florida, neighborhood one night in December 2002. Paul was looking at Christmas lights in the neighborhood and enjoying the cool night air. Foster ambled along beside him. Suddenly, a squirrel crossed their path. Foster took off after the rodent, pulling Paul along behind him. Paul laughed and enjoyed the run. "I was trying to let him think he had a chance to catch the squirrel," he later said.

The squirrel jumped down a small hill into a large metal culvert, or pipe, in a ditch below. Foster stopped short when the squirrel disappeared. Unfortunately for Paul, the teenager couldn't stop as quickly. He flipped over his dog and tumbled down into the ditch. The fall knocked Paul unconscious and left his body draped over the metal pipe, completely hidden from the road in the darkness.

Foster ran down to join Paul and stood beside his injured owner. Every time a car went by, he barked, but no one stopped. The cars whizzed by quickly, unaware that someone was in danger just a few feet away.

Finally, a woman named Kimberly Kemp drove by. As she always did on this stretch of road, Kimberly slowed down, in case a deer or other animal ran out of the darkness. She heard Foster's barking and looked back. There was the dog, still in his leash.

Curious, Kimberly turned back and pulled over. She thought Foster must have run away from his owner, and she tried to grab his leash to bring him into her car. Foster wagged his tail at first, but as soon as Kimberly tried to grab him, he growled.

"What's up with you?" Kimberly asked as another car zoomed by. The car's headlights lit up the scene — and she saw Paul's feet dangling over the side of the culvert. She didn't know if the person were asleep or dead, but she knew she had to get help. She ran back to her car and called 911 on her cell phone.

Police quickly arrived. When an officer shone his flashlight on Paul's face, the victim woke up. He was able to give the police his name so his parents could be called before he was taken to the hospital. He had bruised his spine in the fall but made a complete recovery.

Paul didn't hold any grudges against his dog for causing the accident. "Foster is my best friend," he said. Paul's mother agreed, but commented, "We've just got to fix up Foster with some brake lights!"

SLEEPWALKING SAVIOR

Who would have believed that a little puppy could save a girl's life? For a girl in Lethbridge, Canada, her pet puppy proved to be a lifesaver one bitterly cold winter night.

Sabrina, the eight-year-old daughter of Darren and Lori Holloway, often sleepwalked. Her parents were used to her coming into their room and waking them, and they didn't think much of her nighttime wanderings. That all changed on the night her sleepwalking took her outside. Wearing only her nightgown and a pair of boots, Sabrina let herself out into the yard. Even the bone-chilling air didn't wake up the girl. In her sleepy state, she believed she had to go next door to find her father.

Sabrina didn't know it, but her five-month-old puppy, Pebbles, was alert to her strange behavior. When Pebbles saw Sabrina go outside, she began to howl. Somehow, the puppy knew that she had to wake up Darren and Lori.

Sabrina's parents had never heard Pebbles howl like that before. Finally, at about two o'clock in the morning, Darren got up to let the dog outside. "You must really have to go to the bathroom," he muttered as he opened the door. Then Darren got the shock of his life. There was Sabrina, standing outside on the steps, in temperatures that hovered just above zero.

Darren quickly helped Sabrina inside and put her back to bed. Then he told Lori the whole incredible story. "Pebbles was clearly protecting Sabrina," Darren said. "Just think of what might have happened." She may have lost her way and woken confused, or worst, died of exposure to the cold. Pebbles was a hero for waking up Darren and Lori and alerting them to danger. The family then installed a deadlock, too high for Sabrina to reach, on the front door.

STAY CLOSE TO MY BUDDY

Steven and Ethan were just two boys out on an adventure in the woods one spring day. The eight- and nine-year-old boys ventured into the trees with only Steven's dog, Elmo, a four-year-old Labrador-collie mix, for company. The boys decided to take a trail they hadn't explored before. But the ground turned muddy, and their fun outing turned into a nightmare. The forest had changed into a swamp and the boys soon were completely lost.

Then things got even worse. As the boys and the dog slogged through the mud, Ethan fell. He tried to get up, but he was tangled up in brush and mud. "Steven, help!" he yelled, but Steven wasn't strong enough to pull him out.

"I'm going to get help," Steven said. "Elmo, come on." But the dog refused to budge. "All right, Elmo, you stay with Ethan," Steven told him. Then Steven took off. He plunged through the bushes, his feet slipping in the mud and splashing in the water. Finally, exhausted, terrified, and dripping wet, Steven saw light through the trees. He ran out of the woods, onto a road he recognized, and hurried home. "Mom, Dad, Ethan's in the swamp!" he yelled. "He needs help, quick!"

Steven's parents called the police. Soon the woods were crawling with officers. They even brought in search dogs to help. A helicopter flew overhead, its pilot scanning the ground for any sign of the lost boy. But Steven couldn't retrace his steps and no one could find any trace of Ethan.

The day grew dark and cold as night approached. "We'll have to call off the search until morning," a police officer told Ethan's frantic parents. When Ethan's parents begged them to keep trying, the police agreed to make one more trip into the woods.

As a firefighter walked through the muddy terrain, he switched on his flashlight and swung it in front of him. Suddenly, he stopped. His light had caught the gleam of an animal's eyes. The firefighter walked closer. Then he let out a shout. There, shivering in the water, lay a wet dog and a limp, unconscious boy.

Paramedics rushed Ethan to the hospital. He was treated for hypothermia, or low body temperature, but was home by the next day. Loyal Elmo was also treated by a local vet and soon returned home in perfect health.

"That's some dog you've got there," the police told the boys' parents. "He stayed with Ethan and kept him warm and safe. That boy owes his life to that dog. He's a real hero."

NEVER LEAVE MY SIDE

Chance, a nine-year-old Dalmatian–fox terrier mix, had been a beloved member of the Delorey family of South Bar, Canada, for many years. The dog was especially close to James Delorey. Seven-year-old James was autistic and couldn't speak, but he didn't need words to show how much he loved his spotted dog.

It was an unusually warm December day in 2009, so James's mom, Veronica, decided to let James and Chance play outside. She stood nearby, enjoying the sight of her son and their dog running around the yard.

As she watched, Veronica suddenly heard a loud sound. She looked toward the family's motor home — the large vehicle was rolling slowly down the slope! Somehow, the motor home had slipped into gear, and the brake was off. Veronica ran to the vehicle and jumped in, quickly putting the motor home into park and setting the brake.

"That was close," Veronica exclaimed as she climbed out and headed back to where her son had been playing just moments before. But the boy and his dog were nowhere to be seen. "James! Chance! Where are you?" she yelled. There was no answer. Veronica hurried into the thick woods that bordered the back of their property, calling her son's name over and over. But there was no sign of them.

Veronica ran back to the house and called the police. Soon the forest was filled with rescue crews on four-wheelers and members of the community. A helicopter was even brought in for an overhead look. But the thick trees gave up no secrets. Night fell, and James and Chance had not been found. Veronica was frantic, but one thing helped her feel a little better. "At least Chance is with my son," she said. "I know that he would never leave James alone."

Temperatures plunged overnight and by morning, heavy snow was falling, whipped around by ferocious winds. Searchers kept on, but they could hardly see in the blowing, drifting snow. Veronica couldn't bear to think of her son alone in the snow and cold. He didn't even have a jacket on! All he had was Chance.

The next day, Veronica heard barking. Chance limped out of the woods, barely able to walk in the deep snow. Rescue crews followed Chance's footprints back into the woods. They found the little boy unconscious in the snow. Cold and suffering from frostbite, James was rushed to a hospital. Veronica knew that Chance had kept James warm during the storm. The dog hadn't left his side until the snow stopped and he knew it was time to get help. Chance had lived up to his name, giving James a chance at life.

SUPER SWIMMER!

City life just wasn't right for Echo. The shepherd-collie mix was a stray who found her way into a home in Toronto, Canada. However, Echo's owners could not give the dog the attention or the outdoor space she needed, so they put an ad in the paper to find her a new home.

Echo was adopted by Tish and Ted Smith, who lived on a farm. She loved her new home and spent most of her time outside, herding chickens and cattle and sheep, or simply running through the fields. Most of all, she loved to swim in a pond on the farm. Even though she spent little time inside, she and the Smiths had a strong bond. It wasn't long before Echo's new family found out just how powerful a bond that was.

In July 2006, Tish decided to go on a solo adventure. She and Echo set out for a five-day canoe trip across Lake Huron, the second-largest of the Great Lakes. Tish and Echo enjoyed every minute of their time on the water. Everything was going well until their last day, July 15.

Early that morning, they were in their canoe when a huge thunderstorm roared over the lake. They huddled as enormous waves rocked and tossed their little boat. Echo lay with her head on Tish's thigh, bringing comfort to the brave woman.

The canoe managed to ride out the waves for a while, but Tish's luck didn't last. Another wave flipped the canoe and knocked Tish and Echo into the water. The canoe sank. Only her life jacket kept Tish afloat. She bobbed in the chilly water as Echo swam next to her. There were no other boats in sight. The woman and dog were alone in the middle of the huge lake.

Tish swam or floated in the water for a total of twelve hours. The water temperature plunged as night fell, and so did her body temperature. The last thing she remembered was passing out in the water, Echo still at her side. Only her life jacket kept her head above the water.

Tish awoke hours later in the emergency room. She then found out what had happened. Her partially submerged canoe had been spotted, and Ontario police sent out a search-and-rescue team. They had no idea where Tish might be, or even if she was still in the water. Finally, a rescue helicopter flew close enough to see Echo swimming in circles around Tish's body. The two were quickly rescued and brought to safety.

Perhaps the most amazing part of Tish's rescue was that by the time she was found, she had drifted within sight of the shore. Most dogs in this situation would swim to shore, but not Echo! She went against her natural instincts to protect Tish, staying close to her and maintaining her body temperature by snuggling close and sharing her body heat.

Tish and Echo returned home, where the dog was greeted as a hero. Tish reported that Echo was no longer content to live outside on their farm. Instead, she stayed in the house and followed Tish wherever she went. She even slept on Tish's bed at night! Tish didn't mind one bit.

HORSE SENSE

Lise Sentell was happy. The young woman was about four months pregnant with her first child. One day, Lise went for a ride on Ruby, the horse she'd had since she was a teenager. The two cantered along a trail in the Pennsylvania countryside, several miles from Lise's home. There was no one else on the trail, and Lise was enjoying the peaceful solitude and beautiful scenery.

The day was warm, and Lise felt thirsty. She took a sip from her water bottle. As Ruby trotted along, Lise spied a pond through the trees. She knew Ruby must be thirsty, too, and steered her toward the water's edge so the horse could get a drink. Ruby waded into the cold water and bent her head to drink as Lise sat on her back, waiting for her to finish.

Ruby finished her drink and turned back to wade out of the pond. But the ground was slick and muddy. As Ruby climbed up the bank, her hooves slipped in the mud. Lise screamed as the horse slid back and fell onto her side in the water, trapping Lise's left foot under her heavy body.

Ruby panicked, kicking her legs in the water in an effort to get back to her feet. Lise struggled to free her leg, but her foot was tangled in the stirrup. She ducked as Ruby's hooves nearly hit her. One good kick and Lise knew she could be badly injured. Even worse, the baby inside her could be seriously hurt or even killed.

"Ruby, stop," Lise said. "I'm stuck!" As soon as she heard Lise's voice, Ruby stopped struggling. She lay still as Lise freed her foot and moved out of the way. As soon as Lise got out of the pond, Ruby kicked hard and got to her feet, then carefully walked up onto the bank. The two made their way home, wet, muddy, and sore, but safe.

Five months later, Lise's daughter was born. Ruby continued her gentle ways, and Lise knew her horse would do her best to protect her little girl as well as for Lise for the rest of her life.

A BOY'S BEST FRIEND

When a toddler decided to walk out of the back door of his home one day in Bear, Delaware, it's a good thing the family pet went with him.

Barbara Eckert's two-year-old son, Corey, slipped out of the house in July 2003, followed by the family's golden retriever, Copper. When Barbara realized her son was missing, she called the police, who began to search the wooded area behind her house. Officer Courtney Fry saw the dog running and barking in a field about half a mile away from the house. "I could see the dog in the field going nuts, and I knew the dog was trying to tell us something."

Officer Fry and her partner hurried into the woods. Copper continued "barking his head off," as she put it. Then she heard a boy crying. She and her partner found Corey sitting in the mud. He had slipped and fallen down a deep embankment. The police pulled the boy, who was unharmed but scared, out of the ditch and returned him safely home. Copper led the way. "Copper saved the day," said Officer Fry.

DOG ON DUTY

Falling into a flooded ditch would be terrifying for anyone, but it's even worse if you're disabled and unable to move. That's exactly what happened to Cheryl Smith, who lived in York, the United Kingdom. Fortunately for Cheryl, her dog, Orca, was there to save her.

Cheryl was a twenty-two-year-old college student in May 2003. She used a wheelchair to get around and just five weeks earlier had been matched with Orca, a golden retriever who was trained as an assistance dog. Orca helped Cheryl by pushing buttons at pedestrian crossings and on elevators, opening and closing doors, and turning appliances on and off around the house. But that was nothing compared to what Orca did that May afternoon.

Cheryl was enjoying an afternoon out, riding her wheelchair along a dirt path, with Orca running alongside. Suddenly, the chair struck an object in the path and tipped over. She fell twenty feet down an embankment and landed in a rain-swollen, muddy ditch. To make matters worse, her wheelchair tumbled down the embankment and landed on top of her, pinning her down.

Orca immediately ran for help. At first, Cheryl had little faith that he would come back. "I'd only had him for five weeks, so I did think it was a bit much to expect."

When Orca ran away, Cheryl thought he was gone for good. She started to panic. "I really began to give up hope . . . I was lying there . . . it was pouring with rain and hailstones. There was a foot of water in the ditch, and I was being pushed down into the thick mud below it. I was really scared. I was freezing and knew no one would find me by chance."

Orca, meanwhile, was determined to find help. He spotted Peter Harrison jogging in a nearby field and barked to get his attention. When Peter saw Orca run back and forth between himself and the ditch, he followed to see what was wrong. "As soon as I saw Ms. Smith in the ditch, I yelled that I was getting help," he reported. "I ran home to call the fire department and alert my family. Then I went to meet the fire crew while my wife and daughter hurried back to the ditch." The family stayed with Cheryl until rescuers arrived. Cheryl was taken to the hospital and treated for hypothermia. A few hours later, she and Orca were home, safe and sound.

Orca became a star for what he did that day. In 2006, he received a gold medal from a British organization called PDSA, for bravery and devotion to duty. Cheryl said, "People have described it as a scene from the old Lassie movies." A police officer at the scene explained, "The dog is the real star."

A LIFESAVING WARNING

The Jensen family of Westlock, Canada, had always loved dogs, so they didn't mind taking in a neighbor's dog when she could no longer care for her pet. Patty the border collie was a great addition to the Jensen family farm and often went out into the fields to keep Kai and his son Allan company as they worked around the farm.

One day in May 2009, Kai and Allan went out to prepare their equipment for planting season. The two men checked a machine called an air seeder to make sure it was in good condition. Everything looked great, so Allan climbed into the tractor cab and started the machine. Then he saw something strange.

Patty was jumping up and down against the side of the cab, throwing her black-and-white body against the door. Allan was puzzled. She was usually a quiet dog, and she had never gotten excited about the tractor before. As he sat staring at her, she began running in circles next to the tractor. All the while, she kept looking at Allan and barking.

He jumped out of the cab to see what was wrong. Patty ran behind the tractor, still barking, and he ran after her. To his horror, he saw his father lying under the wheels. Somehow, he had gotten too close as Allan started the engine and fell underneath the six-thousand-pound machine. Allan called 911 from his cell phone, and an ambulance quickly raced to the farm.

Kai suffered serious injuries, but paramedics and a two-month stay in the hospital saved his life. Kai knew he owed his life to Patty, who didn't waste any time and acted like a true hero when danger struck.

AN ICY RESCUE

Mike Hambling liked nothing better than to go for long walks with his dog, Freddie. Freddie was a German shepherd whom Mike and his wife, Debbie, had adopted two years earlier as a puppy. The dog always accompanied Mike on his daily walk around the cottage where they lived in Coldwater, Canada.

One chilly day in late January 2007, Mike and Freddie took their walk around the neighborhood. When they reached the frozen channel near their home, Mike stepped out onto the ice as he had many times before. But this time, Freddie refused to follow. Instead, Freddie pulled on his leash and whined. "Come, boy, let's go," Mike said, with an impatient tug on the leash. Freddie finally followed, walking slowly on the frozen surface.

Suddenly, there was a cracking sound. The ice broke under Mike, and he plunged into the frigid water. He grabbed the edge of the ice and tried to pull himself out, but the thin ice crumbled under his fingers. He began to sink into the water, weighed down by his wet jeans and boots. Mike was so cold, he couldn't think straight. He couldn't move or figure out what to do.

Just then he felt a wrench on his wrist. It was Freddie, pulling on his leash as hard as he could. Debbie was watching from the house, and she ran outside, yelling, "Pull, Freddie, pull!" Freddie pulled with all his might. He dug his paws into the ice and hauled Mike out of the water. Then he dragged his shivering owner back to shore, where Debbie and a neighbor, who had heard her cries, were waiting to help.

"Freddie saved my life, there's no doubt about it," Mike said. From then on, he made sure to heed the dog's warnings about thin ice.

BIG BEAR? NO PROBLEM!

Queenie, a nine-year-old Labrador-shepherd mix, was enjoying a leisurely walk in the park with her owner, Bonnie Pankiw, one day in 2001. As the two walked along the wooded trails, they received a nasty surprise. A full-grown black bear walked right in front of them. Startled and angry, the bear turned and charged at Bonnie. Bonnie jumped back and started to run, but she was no match for the bear. The bear reached her in seconds, and she prepared for the worst.

But the attack never came. Queenie growled and jumped at the bear, biting at its back legs. The bear stopped and backed up, then rushed toward Bonnie again. Once more, Queenie jumped at the bear, barking and snapping at the big attacker. Finally, the bear turned and ran back into the trees.

"Queenie, you're a hero!" Bonnie cried. The Purina Animal Hall of Fame agreed. They inducted Queenie into the Hall of Fame in 2002.

PROTECTING HER YOUNG

A bear attack sounds scary, but what about an attack by a deer? Although these animals seem gentle and shy, an angry deer is dangerous. People have been injured or killed by deer's sharp hooves and dangerous horns. Thanks to a springer spaniel named Holly, little Ally Myers wasn't one of these victims.

One Saturday afternoon in June 1999, four-year-old Ally was walking with her grandmother Norma Myers along a river in Canada. Norma's dog, Holly, came along for company. Ally ran ahead of her grandmother, skipping along and singing.

The noise startled a doe, who may have been protecting her fawn in the trees. The doe ran out of the woods right at Ally, ready to attack. Ally screamed, but something unexpected happened. Before the deer could touch the little girl, Holly jumped between them. She jumped and barked at the deer. Ally ran back to the safety of her grandmother's arms, but Holly paid dearly for her bravery. The deer kicked and stomped on the dog even as she kept barking. Finally, the deer ran back into the woods.

Ally was not injured, but Holly was seriously hurt. Norma rushed her to an animal hospital, where the spaniel had several operations to repair a broken leg and other injuries. She also lost the vision in her right eye in the attack. Just as the angry deer was trying to protect her baby, Holly acted fearlessly to protect a little girl.

CHAPTER 3

IN SICKNESS AND IN HEALTH

An unexpected medical emergency can strike anyone at any time. Fortunately for the people in this chapter, their superhero pets were ready to help when disaster struck.

WAKE UP!

Thelma Portocales was sleeping soundly in her home in Millsboro, Delaware, and thought her husband was sleeping just as soundly beside her. Thelma didn't know that George was in serious trouble — until the family's new dog, Oscar, came to the rescue.

The Portocaleses had gotten Oscar from the Delaware SPCA less than a month earlier. Oscar was a mix of dachshund and schnauzer. He was the first dog the elderly couple had ever owned. Adopting him would turn out to be one of the best things they ever did.

On that September night, Oscar would not stop barking. When Thelma didn't get up, he barked some more. Finally, she got out of bed. That's when she realized that George was not sleeping beside her after all. She wasn't worried. She figured that he must have gotten up to use the bathroom or get a drink of water.

Oscar led Thelma into the bathroom. She turned on the light and peeked in, but saw nothing. "Look, Oscar, there's nothing wrong," she told the little dog. But he knew better. He pushed past her into the bathroom and stood there. Thelma looked down. That's when she saw George lying on the floor. He had suffered a heart attack.

Thelma called 911. Paramedics revived George and rushed him to the hospital. He made a full recovery and was home in a few days. The doctors told her that if Oscar hadn't alerted her, George probably would have died. "Oscar is precious," Thelma said. "He's also one very spoiled dog. George gives him special treatment every day. He just can't get enough of him."

A BOY'S BEST FRIEND

K'os was a gentle giant. This dog, who lived with the Guindon family in Peterborough, Canada, was a Neapolitan mastiff, one of the world's heaviest dog breeds.

But K'os was a sweet and obedient family pet who became a hero one night.

Fourteen-year-old Hunter Guindon was diagnosed with cystic fibrosis in 2009. This serious and chronic disease causes the body to produce too much mucus, making it hard to breathe and digest food. People with cystic fibrosis need special treatments to clear fluid from their lungs and help them breathe.

A few months after Hunter's diagnosis, his parents, Linda and Jason, were asleep when K'os burst into their room, barking loudly and jumping on the bed. The Guindons were surprised and a little scared by the dog's behavior, because he rarely barked. Jason hurried to check the front door, thinking that someone had broken into the house.

K'os didn't follow Jason. Instead, he ran down the hall to Hunter's room and then back to Linda, barking and barking. Linda followed him and turned on the lights. K'os stood over Hunter, who was having a seizure. The teen lay on the floor, his face gray, struggling to breathe. His mouth and throat had filled with mucus and other fluids, and he was choking.

Linda rushed to save her son. She turned Hunter onto his stomach and began wiping fluid from his mouth as she yelled for her husband to call 911. Hunter was rushed to the hospital, where he was treated and released soon afterward. He was diagnosed with epilepsy.

Linda and Jason will never forget what K'os did that night. They truly believed that he saved their son's life. As Hunter faced more health challenges, his parents knew that K'os would be by his side to protect him and keep him safe. After all, that's what heroes do.

COME QUICKLY!

Caleigh, an Irish setter, was always full of energy. Her owner, Max Lovett, who lived near Toronto, Canada, took the dog for a long walk every morning to try to burn off some of her boundless energy. On February 2, 2000, however, Max felt weak. He didn't want his dog to miss her walk, so he had an idea. He and Caleigh drove to a nearby field where she could run off leash while he sat and watched.

Caleigh was having a wonderful time running and jumping in the snow. Max, however, felt worse and worse as the minutes passed. He decided to wait in his car, away from the cold. But as he started back to the car, he suffered a heart attack and collapsed in the snow.

Right away, Caleigh ran to check on her owner. When Max didn't respond, she ran across the field and found Mike Raworth shoveling snow in his driveway. Caleigh jumped at Mike, barking and racing back and forth. Her actions and her pleading stare convinced him that something was wrong, and he rushed to follow her. Finding Max lying unconscious in the snow, Mike ran home to call 911. Then he grabbed a blanket and sat with Max — and Caleigh, too, of course — until help arrived. Max was rushed to the hospital and treated for a heart attack and hypothermia. A local police officer said that Max had survived thanks to the devotion and love Caleigh had for her owner.

NOT SO MELLOW

Mel-O was a cat who lived up to her name. She had been the quietest cat in her litter of kittens, lying meekly in her cage when the Rose family of Edmonton, Canada, came to the animal shelter looking for a new pet in 2005. Nine-year-old Alex picked the quiet kitten and named her for her mellow personality.

Unfortunately, Mel-O became sick with a respiratory virus soon after arriving home. Over the next few weeks, she made many trips to the veterinarian. Alex always went along. He felt a special bond with the sick kitten. Alex had suffered from diabetes since he was a toddler and understood what it felt like to go to the doctor. Diabetes is a disease in which the body cannot produce a chemical called insulin. Insulin regulates the level of sugar in the blood, and too much or too little sugar can make a person very sick. Fortunately for Alex, Mel-O made a complete recovery and was soon back home.

On March 27, 2006, Alex checked his sugar levels and climbed into bed. His parents, Danielle and Sean, went to bed soon afterward. It was only an hour or so later that Alex came into their room. "What are you doing up so late?" Danielle asked.

"Mel-O woke me up," Alex said. "She jumped on my chest and started hitting me in the face with her paws."

"Come on, Alex," Danielle said, thinking this was a joke or an attempt by Alex to stay up past his bedtime. "You know Mel-O never walks on people. How could she even get into your bed?" Alex slept in a top bunk bed, and the only way Mel-O could have gotten up there was to climb the ladder, something else she had never done.

"I don't know, Mom, but that's what happened," Alex said. "I feel fine, but maybe I should check my sugar levels, just in case."

Alex and Danielle went back into the bedroom, where he checked his sugar levels on a special meter. "Mom, look," he said with alarm, showing her the numbers. Danielle gasped. Alex's numbers were dangerously low. If Mel-O had not woken him, he might have had a diabetic seizure that could have killed him.

The Rose family didn't know what triggered Mel-O's lifesaving action that night, but some animals are sensitive to chemical changes in the human body. Whatever the reason, they believe that Mel-O saved Alex's life, just as Alex had saved her life when he adopted her from a shelter.

I WANT MY BREAKFAST!

There was no denying it. Nemo was a fat cat. The twenty-one-pound cat lived with Angela and Peter Papadimitriou in their home in Canada. Nemo loved to eat, and every morning, he woke Peter up for his breakfast.

The plump kitty's routine changed on September 1, 2008. That morning, Nemo went over to Angela's side of the bed instead. He jumped onto the bed, meowing loudly. "Nemo, go away," Angela mumbled. But Nemo began swatting at her face and pushing his head into her arm.

"Peter, go feed the cat," Angela said. "He's driving me crazy." There was no response.. She rolled over. He lay beside her. "Peter, wake up!" she called, getting worried. Still, he didn't answer. She leaned closer and screamed. Peter wasn't breathing!

Angela rushed to call 911. Paramedics arrived and began performing CPR. Peter had suffered a serious heart attack. He was rushed to the hospital, where he underwent heart surgery, and returned home a few weeks later.

Angela knew that if Nemo hadn't been so persistent, she might not have discovered Peter's condition until it was too late. Maybe the fat cat was just impatient for his breakfast that morning, but Angela and Peter believed that their furry friend is a hero.

DOGGIE DIAGNOSIS

Grommett knew something was wrong. His owner, Steve Boyle, of Wakefield, Rhode Island, had not been feeling well, and the six-year-old golden retriever was worried. "He would circle and circle around me, getting under my feet," Steve said. "And then he would lean on me. He made me so uncomfortable that I decided to go to the hospital." Steve's doctors discovered that a virus had infected his heart, making it swell and not work properly. If Steve hadn't gotten medical help, his heart could have failed completely.

Steve recovered and said that Grommett had sensed illness in people before. Some time ago, Steve's son, Francis, wasn't feeling well. He finally went for a blood test after Grommett circled around him as if he were herding sheep. It turned out the college student had a disease called mononucleosis and needed medical attention. The Boyles also said that Grommett seemed to know when a visitor was sick and would rest his head in the visitor's lap as if to comfort him or her.

Steve was not really a dog lover before Grommett saved his life. That all changed, and Grommett became his constant companion. "He's the first dog that's ever really gotten to me," Steve said. "He really wormed his way into my heart."

Grommett lived with the Boyles for twelve years, until he passed away in 2009. He truly was his man's best friend.

KINDRED SPIRITS

Twelve-year-old Jordan Haag had his diabetes under control, or so he thought. But one night in May 2003, Jordan's diabetes almost killed him — until his dog, Jed, came to the rescue.

The Haags were asleep in their house in Fond du Lac, Wisconsin, when disaster struck. Jordan's blood sugar dropped alarmingly low, and he went into convulsions in his bed. No one realized what was happening — no one except for Jed.

Jed jumped on Jordan's bed and began barking. Jordan's parents ran to see what was wrong. When Jill saw Jordan convulsing, she called 911. Paramedics arrived and ordered Jed out of the room so the dog wouldn't get in their way. But Jed refused to leave. Instead, he slipped under Jordan's bed and waited quietly while rescuers gave Jordan medicine and got him ready for a trip to the hospital.

Fortunately, Jordan recovered quickly and was back at school a few days later. But his family knew that things could have turned out differently if Jed hadn't alerted them.

Oddly enough, Jordan wasn't the first member of the Haag family to suffer a seizure. Jed had them, too. The dog had epilepsy and suffered several seizures every year. "Jed knows when he has a seizure himself," Jill said. "I don't know if he recognized it when Jordan had the seizure."

Whatever the reason for his awareness, Jed became Jordan's constant companion after his seizure. While he used to sleep on Jill's bed, he moved to the foot of Jordan's bed after that frightening night. "It has been a very special thing," she reported. "Ever since it happened, Jed just sits and watches him."

A PERFECT PIG

Many people enjoy the companionship of an unusual pet — the potbellied pig. These pets are clean and smart, and they can grow to weigh up to two hundred pounds. That intelligence and large size made one special pig named Lulu a hero.

Lulu lived with her owner, Jo Ann Altsman. In August 1998, Jo Ann was alone in her trailer home when she suffered a serious heart attack. Somehow, Lulu sensed something was wrong and knew that Jo Ann needed help. But how could a pig call for help? The big pig did the only thing she could do. Lulu walked outside and lay in the road.

It wasn't long before a man drove down the road and had to stop for the piggy barricade. "Hey, pig, get out of my way," he yelled. Lulu didn't budge. The driver blew his horn and yelled some more, but Lulu just lay there, looking at him. There was no way he could drive past a 150-pound pig and no room in the narrow street to turn around and drive away. He was stuck . . . unless he could figure out what Lulu wanted.

The driver got out of the car, and Lulu stood up. She walked toward Jo Ann's trailer, grunting. Puzzled, he followed Lulu into the house. He saw Jo Ann lying on the floor and realized she needed help. He called 911, and Jo Ann was rushed to the hospital.

Doctors at the hospital told Jo Ann that if she had reached the hospital merely fifteen minutes later, she might not have survived. A grateful Jo Ann treated her beloved pig to a jelly doughnut as a reward for saving her life.

BELLE ON THE CELL

Dialing a phone to call for help is amazing if you're an animal, but how about calling for help on a *cell phone*? That's just what Belle, the beagle, did when her owner suffered a life-threatening diabetic seizure.

For Kevin Weaver of Orlando, Florida, Belle was more than just a pet. She's a medical helper. Dogs are sensitive to smell and many can even detect changes in body chemistry caused by a dangerous change in blood-sugar levels. Belle had been specially trained to alert Kevin of this. "Every time she paws at me like that, I grab my meter and test myself," he reported. "She's never been wrong."

Kevin also taught Belle a special trick. He showed her how to dial 9 on his cell phone. Dialing 9 was his speed-dial code for 911. When he suffered his diabetic seizure in 2006, she knew just what to do. She found his cell phone and bit down on the number 9. Paramedics arrived quickly and brought Kevin to the hospital for treatment. "There is no doubt in my mind that I'd be dead if I didn't have Belle," he said.

Belle received a special award for her actions. In June of 2006, she and Kevin traveled to Washington, DC, to receive a VITA Wireless Samaritan Award. This award is given every year to someone who uses a cell phone to save a life or prevent a crime. Belle was the first dog to ever receive the award.

OVERCOMING HER FEARS

Gary and Vickie Ritter had owned their golden retriever, Ginger, for many years, and they knew their dog well. One thing they knew for sure was that Ginger hated loud noises. "Anytime someone was causing a loud noise, she either went to the other side of the house or inside the house if she could," Gary explained. Airplanes, lawn mowers, truck engines — it didn't matter. Ginger hated them all.

Ginger also hated rattlesnakes, which were plentiful in their desert neighborhood. "If one came in the yard, we could tell it by Ginger's frantic movements to get inside," Gary said. He didn't think anything of it. After all, getting away from a rattlesnake is a smart thing to do.

One day, everything changed. Vickie was mowing the lawn, and Ginger, of course, was hiding on the far side of the house, away from the noise. But when Vickie came around the side of the house, Ginger suddenly ran and stood in front of her, blocking her path, instead of avoiding the mower. Vickie moved it closer, thinking Ginger would run out of the way, but the dog stood her ground. Then the dog did something even more unusual. She dove at something next to the house. Her head jerked back, and Vickie saw a rattlesnake strike.

The snake bit Ginger twice in the face. Vickie turned off the mower and yelled for Gary, who ran over with a shovel. He killed the snake, then grabbed Ginger and rushed her to the vet. Sadly, the venom was too powerful. The vet sent Ginger home, where she died a few days later.

Gary and Vickie still missed their dog. Gary said, "There is not a doubt in my mind that Ginger laid down her life for Vickie. . . . She knew the snake was there, she was afraid of snakes and lawn mowers, but she stood just five feet from a mower and took the snakebite herself."

THE HEIMLICH DOG?

There are many stories about dogs rescuing people from fires or attacks from other animals. But have you ever heard of a dog who saved its owner from choking? That's what Toby, a two-year-old golden retriever, did.

Toby's owner, Debbie Parkhurst, was eating an apple at her home in Calvert, Maryland, when a piece of the fruit got stuck in her throat. Debbie tried to force the apple out of her throat by giving herself the Heimlich maneuver, but her efforts didn't work. The Heimlich maneuver is used to save people from choking by placing pressure on the lower chest to dislodge an object blocking the airway. Frantic, she began pounding on her chest. That's when Toby heard her choking and ran in to help her. "The next thing I know, Toby's up on his hind feet and he's got his front paws on my shoulders," Debbie recalled. He knocked her to the floor and then jumped up and down on her chest. The force of his jumps dislodged the apple and saved her life. "I literally have paw print–shaped bruises on my chest," Debbie told reporters, but she didn't mind one bit. For his actions, Toby received the ASPCA Dog of the Year Award in 2007.

CHAPTER 4

GOOD NEIGHBORS

It's one thing for a pet to save its own family. But some animals give new meaning to the phrase *good neighbor*! Here are stories of superhero pets who saved the lives of people they didn't even know.

A CHANGE OF PLAN

Corey was a miniature schnauzer who had won prizes in dog shows all over the United States and Canada. By the time he was fourteen years old, he had retired and lived a relaxing life with his owner, Jay Sobel, in North York, Canada. A daily walk through the neighborhood was about all the excitement Corey had — until one day when he sensed danger and saved a neighbor's life.

Corey always walked the same route during his daily exercise. So Jay was surprised when the dog changed his path on a warm day in May 2007. The neighborhood was busy that day. Boys and girls played in their yards and rode bikes in the street. Other neighbors mowed their lawns or worked on their cars. Corey walked along, looking at everything around him.

When Jay and Corey reached the corner, Jay started to turn left as they always did. But Corey had other ideas. He bolted to the right and almost dragged Jay down the sidewalk. Suddenly, Jay heard a weak voice calling, "Help me! I can't breathe! Help!" Corey stopped in front of a fence, and Jay peered inside. He saw a man in the deep end of a pool, hanging on to the edge for dear life.

Jay and Corey rushed to the pool, where Jay carefully lifted the man out of the water. Eighty-year-old Jack Turner had been inspecting the pool when he got dizzy and fell in. The elderly man had a serious respiratory disease called emphysema, and could hardly catch his breath after Jay pulled him out. Jay helped the man into a chair and left Corey to keep him company while he ran into the house to call 911. Paramedics gave Jack oxygen and rushed him to the hospital, where he was treated for emphysema and a mild heart attack, as well as for serious cuts on his hands where he had scraped them trying to lift himself out of the pool.

Jack soon returned home. After that day, Corey changed his routine to pass the Turners' house every day to receive a pat on the head from his new friend.

AN EAR FOR DANGER

Samuri's life got off to a rough start. The Akita was the smallest and weakest of his mother's litter of puppies. Still, he seemed like the perfect dog to the Drozdowski family of Winnipeg, Canada. Soon after they adopted Samuri, they realized their new dog was blind. Samuri's disability only made Don and Jo-Ann love him more. They soon discovered that although Samuri couldn't see, his hearing was as sharp as any dog's.

One cold night in 2005, Don and Jo-Ann were watching television inside the house. Samuri was outside in the yard. Suddenly, he began barking so loudly that the Drozdowskis could hear him over the television. Samuri had barked at things in the yard before, but this time, his bark was urgent and demanding. Don decided to go outside and see what was wrong. "It's probably just someone walking down the sidewalk," he said as he pulled on his winter coat.

Don stepped outside. Samuri was barking at the edge of their yard, his attention focused across the street. Don saw a dark shape against the curb. He rushed over and realized the shape was his neighbor, Kathy Arnold. The college student was lying in the road, calling weakly for help. The sound was barely audible — except to Samuri's sharp ears.

Don rushed back inside and yelled for Jo-Ann to call 911 and Kathy's parents. Neighbors gathered and watched as an ambulance rushed Kathy to the hospital. She had suffered a stroke but would recover.

Kathy's mother, Eileen, would never forget the night Samuri saved her daughter's life. "I'm so thankful that Samuri was watching out, or should I say, listening out, for my daughter," she told reporters. "He was her guardian angel that night."

FOLLOW ME!

It was just an ordinary day for the Andrews family of Canada in 1997. They were at home with their dog, Morphy, a three-year-old yellow Labrador. Suddenly, Morphy ran to the door and barked. Esther let him outside, thinking he just wanted a quick walk. Instead, he pulled at her sleeve to force her outside.

"Morphy, where are you going?" Esther called as she tried to keep up with her dog. He was in a big hurry. He ran around a fifty-foot-long cedar hedge at the edge of the Andrewses' property, then streaked across the neighbor's yard and onto the porch.

Esther ran behind her dog, wondering what he was doing. When she got to the porch, she saw her neighbor Doug Rogers slumped in a chair. "My chest hurts. I can't breathe," the elderly man said. She called 911, and paramedics quickly brought Doug to the hospital. He'd been sitting outside when he suffered a heart attack. Only Morphy had heard his weak cries for help from across the yard and in the house. He saved Doug's life that day.

GIVING HIS LIFE FOR OTHERS

George was just an ordinary Jack Russell terrier, who lived with his owner, Alan Gay, in New Zealand. George was a popular dog in the neighborhood and often played with the local children. But no one thought that George was a hero until one sad day in April 2007.

On that day, George was strolling with a group of children. He accompanied them to a store and waited outside while they bought some candy. As they walked home, they were suddenly attacked by two pit bulls. As the children screamed, George rushed to help. Despite his small size, he fearlessly barked at the pit bulls, trying to chase them away. Richard Rosewarne, one of the children, recalled that "George tried to protect us by barking and rushing at them, but they started to bite him. One bit him on the head, and the other on the back."

The children were able to run away. They were uninjured, and the pit bulls were found later and turned over to the police. Sadly, George was badly hurt. Alan rushed the dog to the vet, but the little dog had to be put to sleep because of his serious injuries.

George's bravery became famous all over New Zealand, Australia, and as far away as the United States. The PDSA awarded him its coveted PDSA Gold Medal, and a statue of George was built in town. A Vietnam War veteran named Jerrell Hudman sent him one of the Purple Hearts he had won in combat, because he was so moved by "the little warrior," as he called him. Most of all, George lives on as an example of bravery and selflessness for the five children he protected that day.

HELPING A FRIEND

Sara Whalen never wanted a pet. She never had any pets when she was growing up, and her parents told her that animals were dirty and belonged outside. It wasn't until a stray dog saved her son that Sara's attitude about animals changed.

Sara, her husband, and their one-and-a-half-year-old son, Adam, lived in upstate New York. An elderly lady lived next door with her golden retriever, Brandy. Little Adam loved Brandy and often ran over to pet the dog when he saw her outside. Sara didn't mind — as long as Brandy stayed outside.

One day, Brandy's owner died. Her relatives came and cleaned out her house, then chased Brandy outside, locked the doors, and left. The abandoned dog relied on neighbors for food and shelter. Sara didn't want any responsibility for the dog, and she certainly didn't want to adopt her and bring her into her home.

Then one day, Adam disappeared. He'd been playing outside in the yard, but when Sara went to check on him, he was gone. Frantic, she called the police. She and her neighbors began to search. When the police arrived, they fanned into the woods behind the house, calling and searching for hours. But there was no sign of Adam anywhere.

Suddenly, one of Sara's neighbors remembered the dog. "Where's Brandy?" she asked.

"Who cares about Brandy?" Sara said. "I just want to find Adam!"

"Maybe she's with Adam," another person said.

A police officer overheard them talking. "I heard a dog barking in the woods," he said. "Let's check it out."

Everyone rushed into the woods, calling Brandy's name. From far away, they heard a faint bark. They moved toward the sound and hurried through the trees. Then they stopped, unable to believe their eyes.

Adam was leaning against a tree trunk, fast asleep. Standing behind him, with her shoulder pressed against his back, was Brandy. One of her legs hung over a steep drop to a stream thirty-five feet below. If Brandy had moved, Adam could have fallen into the stream and drowned.

Sara rushed to grab Adam out of harm's way. As soon as Adam was safe, Brandy collapsed on the ground, exhausted from hours of keeping Adam out of danger. "She must have followed Adam when he wandered off . . . and she saw danger," Sara later explained. "She was a better mother than I [was]; she'd pushed him out of harm's way — and held him there."

A police officer carried Adam home, and Sara carried Brandy. "I knew in that instant that Brandy was coming home with me, too," she said. Brandy lived with the family for the rest of her long life.

As for Sara, her attitude about pets changed. Inspired by Brandy, she not only welcomed animals into her home, she started a rescue group for unwanted golden retrievers who might otherwise have been put to sleep. "If someone had put an abandoned, eleven-year-old golden retriever to sleep twenty-nine years ago, I would not have a child," she explained. Brandy changed everything.

A LUCKY BREAK

House painter Kevin McDonald was standing on the roof of a home in Akron, Ohio, twelve feet above the ground, when disaster struck. The ladder he was standing on suddenly collapsed. "Once the ladder broke, that was it. I was on the ground so fast, I had no time to react," Kevin later said.

Bleeding and badly hurt, Kevin wondered if anyone would help him. The owner of the house was away at work, and he knew that no one could see him from the road. Luckily for him, however, someone was home — the family pet, Ivan, a golden retriever. Ivan ran to check on him, then ran across the yard, barking.

Neighbor Marie Istvan heard the commotion and went outside. "The dog acted real funny, like there was something wrong," she said. Marie followed Ivan back home, where she found Kevin lying on the ground. She called 911 and Kevin was rushed to the hospital.

The painter returned to work a few weeks later. Before he finished painting, he had something important to do. He gave Ivan a treat to thank him!

OLD FRIENDS

Jeb Hurt wondered what on earth was going on. His golden retriever, Stony, wouldn't stop barking. Finally, Jeb went out to see what was wrong. Stony ran next door to their neighbor Clarence Bell's house. Jeb followed.

Clarence was ninety-four years old and lived alone in his house in Beaumont, Texas. The elderly man enjoyed visits from Stony. "We've been big buddies for the last nine years," Clarence said. On that fateful day, he had fallen in his driveway and broken his hip. Unable to move, he was glad to see Stony run over to visit. Stony laid his head on Clarence's chest and looked at him, as if to ask why he was lying on the pavement.

"Stony," Clarence had said, "go get some help. I'm hurt." The dog jumped up and ran home, barking loudly the whole way. Soon afterward, he was back with Jeb, who called 911. "If it hadn't been for that dog, I don't know how long I'd have lay there," Clarence said.

Jeb was stunned by his dog's heroic actions. "I didn't know he had it in him," he said. "He's never been faced with anything like this before. He's the best dog in the world. . . . I wouldn't trade him for anything." Neither would Clarence.

CHAPTER 5

THE BEST THERAPY

Animals have been used as guides and for services for many years. Some pets have a special role — they give comfort and love to people who are sick, lonely, or afraid. Meet some superhero therapy pets who help make the world a better place for the people who need them most.

A FRIEND FOR ALL

Brown Bear was in trouble — big trouble. The big mutt was just days away from being euthanized at an animal shelter in Washington, DC. Then the dog found some guardian angels. A rescue group, called Lucky Dog Animal Rescue, adopted Brown Bear and acquired him a new home. The lucky dog went to live at the Brooke Grove Rehabilitation and Nursing Center in Sandy Grove, Maryland.

Brown Bear's new family included 168 residents at the center. Most of the residents are elderly and many have a disease called dementia that makes them confused and unable to remember things. Brown Bear was a comfort to these residents. If someone was upset or confused, Brown Bear would be there to calm him or her.

Brown Bear didn't have just human friends in his new home. The nursing center also had another dog, two cats, and several birds, all of whom provided comfort to the residents. "Life is enhanced by the ability to walk through a building and be able to pet a dog's muzzle or snuggle a cat," said Brooke Grove's coordinator. Brown Bear was a hero at making people feel better.

PURR THERAPY

Cats can be healers, too. Jak was a sphynx cat who worked as a therapy pet. Sphynx cats are unusual because they don't have any hair, but they can have a lot of love.

Jak belonged to Terry and Sharron True. Sharron was a nurse and Terry was a doctor in Muscle Shoals, Alabama. Every week, the Trues would take Jak to visit patients at a rehabilitation center. Patients spend many weeks and months at the center, recovering from injuries, strokes, or serious illnesses. It's hard for them to be away from their families for so long, and they miss their pets, too.

Jak would bring comfort to the patients in a simple way. He would curl up on their laps and stay there. Some patients would talk to the cat, while others were happy to pet him or just let him sit with them. Terry said that Jak's hairless body felt like soft velvet, and holding him was like "holding a suede hot water bottle." The patients at the center just knew that holding Jak would make them feel much better.

SURF THERAPY

Judy Fridono had big plans for her new dog, Ricochet. She wanted the puppy to be a service dog for people with disabilities. She enrolled Ricochet in a training program, and at first, Ricochet was a star. But things changed as the puppy grew older. "She liked to chase birds," Judy explained, "and that could be harmful for someone with disabilities."

Judy tried her best to change Ricochet's behavior, but the dog wouldn't stop her wild ways. Finally, Judy realized that Ricochet just wasn't cut out to be a service dog. "I tried for months to make her something she wasn't, but finally had to release her from the program," she admitted.

Judy decided to let Ricochet do what she wanted, rather than forcing her to give up her playful nature. The family lived in Southern California, where surfing is a popular sport. Ricochet loved to surf, so Judy spent many hours holding a surfboard in the water so her dog could leap on board and catch a wave.

One day in August 2009, Ricochet was surfing next to Patrick Ivison, a teenager who was quadriplegic, or paralyzed in all four limbs. Suddenly, Ricochet jumped off her surfboard and onto Patrick's board. The two rode the waves into shore. Patrick loved the experience and asked if Ricochet would surf with him again. The pair of surfers had fun, and Judy had a great idea. She could combine Ricochet's love of surfing with her own desire to have the dog help others. Ricochet became a surfing buddy, or a "SURFice" dog for disabled surfers.

Since that day, Ricochet surfed with disabled teens, children, and adults. She sat on the board, which helps the surfer keep his or her balance and gives the surfer something to hold on to. Judy has also held several fund-raisers featuring Ricochet, and the pair has raised more than $125,000 for medical treatment and equipment. In 2011, the ASPCA gave Ricochet its Dog of the Year award for her ability to help others while catching just the right wave.

A SOLDIER'S FRIEND

War can do terrible things to people. Some soldiers who return from combat suffer from a condition called post-traumatic stress disorder, or PTSD. PTSD makes people anxious, angry, and depressed. PTSD sufferers have trouble sleeping and coping with everyday situations. It is important for these victims to receive treatment by mental-health professionals. Believe it or not, some of the best mental-health therapy comes from dogs. One of these dogs was Stinky, a rottweiler who lived in Winnipeg, Canada.

Stinky's original name was Nikki, but after a run-in with a pair of skunks, she got a new name. Stinky was the lead dog in a unique program called the Manitoba Search and Rescue's Elite Psychiatric Therapy Dog Program. Dogs in this program are specially chosen for their intelligence and friendliness. These dogs are trained to work as psychiatric service dogs, providing companionship and affection to soldiers suffering from PTSD.

Stinky provided support to soldiers who need to learn to trust again. Many soldiers said that Stinky saved their lives by giving them hope and the will to go on. In 2011, Stinky was honored for her work when she was inducted into the Purina Animal Hall of Fame.

THE MOST FAMOUS DOG IN ENGLAND

Endal the Labrador retriever was one of the world's most famous superhero pets. This service-and-therapy dog achieved global fame and was filmed by television and movie crews. His achievement: helping his owner live a normal life.

Endal began training to be a therapy dog when he was just a puppy. At first, Endal's owners weren't sure he could be a therapy dog. He was born with a serious joint condition that affected his front legs and made it hard for him to walk. His owners worked hard to find a diet and exercise program that would help him, and their efforts paid off. Endal was certified as an assistance dog. Soon afterward, he was assigned to an ex–Royal Navy officer named Allen Parton.

Allen had suffered serious head injuries during the Gulf War. He had severe memory and visual-perception problems and was confined to a wheelchair. When he first was partnered with Endal, Allen was unable to speak and had to communicate through hand signals. He was also depressed and felt isolated because of his injuries.

When you are disabled, even ordinary tasks can be extremely difficult. Endal helped Allen in many ways. The dog learned to retrieve items from supermarket shelves, operate buttons and switches, open doors, and load and empty the washing machine. One of his most amazing tasks was working an ATM. In total, Endal could respond to hundreds of voice and sign-language commands. Whatever Allen needed, Endal could do.

Endal's training saved Allen's life several times. Allen sometimes suffered seizures. If this occurred while he was in the bathtub, he could have drowned. Endal knew how to pull the plug to drain the bathwater, push Allen into a sitting position, and call for help by hitting an emergency button on the phone.

Endal's most remarkable rescue occurred in 2001, when Allen was knocked out of his wheelchair by a car that passed too close. Endal pushed Allen into a recovery position, covered him in a blanket, fetched his cell phone, and then ran to a nearby hotel and barked until someone came out to help.

Endal also aided Allen in other ways. Allen credits Endal with helping him believe he could have a normal life despite his severe disabilities. The two shared a close bond. Endal even gave Allen his voice back. Allen told a reporter that he and Endal lived in a silent world, communicating only through signs and gestures. Then one day, Allen grunted. Endal was beside himself with joy. "That was like an electric shock going through him, he was so excited," Allen said. "They said I'd never speak again, but Endal just dragged the speech out of me."

Allen wanted everyone to know how special his partner was. Through Allen's efforts, Endal became known all over England and around the world. Television crews came to Allen's house to film Endal and Allen going about their daily routine. Endal also won a number of awards for his work, including the PDSA's Gold Medal for Animal Gallantry and Devotion to Duty, which is the highest award available to an animal. In addition, Allen wrote a book about Endal, which became a bestseller and is in the process of being turned into a movie.

Allen wished he could keep Endal forever, but the dog was getting old, and his health was failing. To make sure he would never be alone, Allen used Endal to help train a puppy, named Endal Junior, to take over Endal's work. Finally, in March 2009, Endal passed away.

Allen wanted Endal's example to help others. In February 2010, he started a charity called Hounds for Heroes. This charity helps train service dogs to support men and women who are injured in the armed forces. He's sure Endal would approve.

CHAPTER 6

WILD HEROES

We've seen that cats, dogs, pigs, and other domestic animals can be heroes. But pets aren't the only superheroes in the animal world. Although wild animals are often dangerous, there have been some surprising stories of wild animals' coming to people's aid.

SUPER SEAL!

Hugh Ryono loved his volunteer job at the Marine Mammal Care Center at Fort MacArthur, California. One of his favorite assignments was taking care of the elephant seals. Whenever he made his rounds, he was always accompanied by Gimpy, a seal pup weighing more than 150 pounds. Hugh knew that even though Gimpy was sweet, elephant seals can be aggressive and dangerous. That's why he always carried a board to protect himself in case one of the other seals attacked.

One day, as Hugh was making his rounds, something unexpected happened. He slipped on a sardine left on the deck of the pool. He fell hard, landing on his stomach and losing his wind. For a few seconds, he couldn't catch his breath. As he looked up, dazed, he saw a terrifying sight. Three elephant seals were rushing toward him, yelping. Hugh knew that they were about to attack. He fumbled for his board and struggled to stand up on the slippery deck.

Just then Hugh saw Gimpy. The seal pup rushed to Hugh's side, opening her mouth menacingly at the other seals. As they moved closer to Hugh, she blocked their path and forced them back. Hugh got to his feet and hurried to safety as Gimpy kept the other seals away from him. "She became my shield," he later said. "She saved me from a mauling that day — there's no doubt about it."

BELUGA TO THE RESCUE!

Yang Yun took part in a dangerous sport called free diving. Little did the Chinese diver know that on one of her dives, her life would be saved — by a whale!

In 2009, Yun was taking part in a free-diving competition at an aquarium in Polar Land, in Harbin, China. Competitors had to sink to the bottom of the aquarium's twenty-foot-deep pool and stay there as long as possible, without wearing an oxygen tank or any other equipment. What made the contest even more challenging was that the water was kept at freezing temperatures because the pool was home to a group of beluga whales.

Yun sank to the bottom and stayed there as long as she could. But when she went to push herself up to the surface, she discovered, to her horror, that her legs had cramped up from the cold water. She couldn't move at all. "I began to choke and sank even lower, and I thought that was it for me — I was dead. Until I felt this incredible force under me driving me to the surface," Yun later told news reporters. That "incredible force" was Mila, a beluga whale. The whale gently grabbed Yun's leg and guided her safely to the surface.

Contest organizers and aquarium staff were stunned by Mila's lifesaving rescue. "We suddenly saw the girl being pushed to the top of the pool with her leg in Mila's mouth," an organizer explained. "She's a sensitive animal who works closely with humans, and I think this girl owes Mila her life." Sometimes, it seems that a whale can be a diver's best friend.

DOLPHINS SAVE THE DAY

Todd Endris believed in miracles. That's because he was alive thanks to one. He was saved from a shark attack by a pod of dolphins.

Todd was surfing with some friends in the waters off Marina State Beach in Monterey, California. He was sitting on his surfboard when a twelve- to fifteen-foot-long shark came out of nowhere and knocked him off his board. The shark then grabbed him around his midsection, ripping the skin off his back as if it were "a banana peel." Luckily, Todd was able to grab his surfboard to his body, so the shark couldn't bite his stomach or chest. But he was bleeding heavily and was helpless in the water.

Then the shark came in for another attack. It grabbed Todd's right leg and chomped it to the bone. Somehow, Todd managed to kick the shark away with his other leg, but he knew the predator would be back for more.

That's when a miracle happened. A pod of dolphins circled the injured swimmer, keeping the shark from coming back. The dolphins continued to protect Todd until he could crawl onto his board and float back to shore. His friends quickly gave him emergency first aid and called for help, and soon he was airlifted to the hospital. After months of healing and therapy, Todd was finally able to get back into the water and resume the sport he loved. And whenever he saw a dolphin, he felt a rush of gratitude.

KEEPING SWIMMERS SAFE

Todd Endris is not the only swimmer who was saved from a shark attack by dolphins. Other swimmers have had similar experiences. In New Zealand, a pod of dolphins made sure a shark didn't have a chance to hurt anyone.

It was a beautiful summer day in Whangarei, New Zealand, perfect for an afternoon swim. Rob Howes brought his daughter, Niccy, and two of his colleagues to Ocean Beach. The four were lifeguard training in the surf when something unusual happened.

"Dad, look at the dolphins," Niccy said. Rob turned and saw a group of dolphins swimming toward them. He'd seen dolphins at this beach before, but never so close. And the dolphins were getting closer!

"Dad, they want to swim with us!" she cried in delight as the dolphins formed a ring around them. He wasn't so sure. The dolphins were behaving strangely, swimming in circles around them. They came so close that the swimmers had to back up until they were huddled together in a tight circle.

"Let's get to shore," Rob said. He started to swim away from the others, but one big dolphin quickly moved in front of him and this pushed him back. Rob felt as if he were a sheep being herded. "This is crazy," he said.

Just then Rob saw another form moving through the water. This time, it wasn't a dolphin — it was a ten-foot-long shark, and it was heading right toward them! "Stay here!" he said. "The dolphins are keeping us safe."

For forty long minutes, Rob, Niccy, and the other lifeguards stayed in the dolphin ring. The shark kept coming toward them, but each time it got near, the dolphins slapped their tails on the water to chase it away. Finally, the deadly shark lost interest and swam off. Only then did the dolphins open their ring and allow the swimmers to swim back to shore.

Rob's story made the newspapers, which was confirmed by a lifeguard who had been patrolling in a boat and seen the whole amazing event. Ingrid Visser, of an environmental group called Orca Research, said the dolphins' behavior made perfect sense. In the wild, she explained, dolphins circle their young to protect them from sharks. "They could have sensed the danger to the swimmers and taken action to protect them," she said.

A SWIMMER'S FRIEND

Davide Ceci couldn't swim, but back in the summer of 2000, the fourteen-year-old was enjoying a day out on his father's boat off the coast of southeastern Italy. The fun day almost turned tragic when Davide accidentally fell off the boat and into the deep waters of the Adriatic Sea, without anyone in his family seeing what had happened.

Davide was drowning when a dolphin, named Filippo by local residents, came to the rescue. Filippo pushed Davide up and out of the water. Davide grabbed on to the dolphin and let the animal tow him through the water. Filippo swam close enough to the family's boat for Davide's father to see him and pull his son to safety.

Davide's mother called Filippo a hero. "It seems impossible an animal could have done something like that, to feel the instinct to save a human life," she said. Filippo had lived in nearby waters for several years after becoming separated from a school of dolphins. He had no fear of people and had always been a favorite of tourists. Filippo became a favorite of the Ceci family after his lifesaving efforts that day!

A MOTHER'S INSTINCT

Gorillas have a reputation as intelligent animals who take good care of their babies. However, these animals also are large and strong and can seriously injure or even kill humans. They are wild animals, not pets. However, that doesn't mean a gorilla can't help a little boy in trouble.

On August 16, 1996, a family was visiting the gorilla exhibit at the Brookfield Zoo in Chicago, Illinois. A three-year-old boy in the group wanted a closer look at the gorillas. When his parents weren't looking, he climbed over the wall, then fell twenty feet onto the concrete floor below. The boy was knocked out by the fall and lay helplessly, just a few feet away from the wild gorillas.

As spectators watched in horror, several gorillas approached the unconscious boy. Just then Binti Jua, a young mother gorilla, pushed through the group. She carried her own baby on her back. As amazed onlookers watched, she gently picked up the injured boy and moved him about sixty feet to the entrance of the exhibit. Zookeepers were able to grab the boy and pull him to safety. After a checkup at the hospital, the boy was released. And Binti Jua joined the list of animals whose compassion saved a human life.

JAMBO CARES

Binti Jua was not the first gorilla to show concern for a human child. A similar incident occurred at the Jersey Zoo in the United Kingdom. A gorilla named Jambo became famous after he performed an amazing deed on August 31, 1986. On that day, five-year-old Levan Merritt fell into the gorilla enclosure and was knocked unconscious. Onlookers watched in horror as other gorillas started to approach the helpless boy. Then something astonishing happened. Just like Binti Jua, Jambo stepped between the helpless boy and the gorillas so none of the animals could touch him. He even comforted the boy by stroking him gently.

In time, the boy regained consciousness. When he saw the gorilla standing over him, Levan started to cry. The sound made Jambo and the other gorillas nervous. Still, they didn't try to hurt Levan. Instead, Jambo led the other gorillas into a small house in the enclosure, allowing zookeepers to enter and safely rescue Levan. The boy was taken to a hospital and made a full recovery.

Meanwhile, Jambo's story was being filmed by a zoo visitor named Brian Le Lion, and it became a sensation around the world. Television stations and newspapers featured the story, which helped people better understand the gentle nature of gorillas.

Jambo died of natural causes in 1992. The Jersey Zoo erected a bronze statue of him inside the zoo grounds as a tribute to the gorilla who showed people that wild animals can be heroes, too.

ABOUT THE AUTHOR

Joanne Mattern grew up along the banks of the Hudson River in New York State, in a family and neighborhood that was full of pets. An avid reader growing up, she worked as an editor for several children's book publishers before becoming a writer. Joanne is the author of many nonfiction books for children, including many on science and nature topics. She also works in a library and loves being surrounded by books all day! Joanne lives in New York State with her husband, four children, and an assortment of pets that includes a dog, cats, geckos, goldfish, and a turtle.

FOR MORE TRUE STORIES OF HEROIC ANIMALS BY JOANNE MATTERN, DON'T MISS *WAR DOGS*.